D0689773

America's Oddest

LAWS

Weird America!

By Michael Canfield

Gareth Stevens
PUBLISHING

Please visit our website, www.garethstevens.com. For a free color catalog of all our high-quality books, call toll free 1-800-542-2595 or fax 1-877-542-2596.

Library of Congress Cataloging-in-Publication Data

Canfield, Michael, 1977- author.
 America's oddest laws / Michael Canfield.
     pages cm. — (Weird America!)
 Includes index.
ISBN 978-1-4824-4027-0 (pbk.)
ISBN 978-1-4824-4028-7 (6 pack)
ISBN 978-1-4824-4029-4 (library binding)
1. Law—United States—Humor. 2. Law—United States—Miscellanea. I. Title.
 K184.C36 2016
 349.73—dc23

                        2015035890

First Edition

Published in 2016 by
Gareth Stevens Publishing
111 East 14th Street, Suite 349
New York, NY 10003

Copyright © 2016 Gareth Stevens Publishing

Designer: Sarah Liddell
Editor: Ryan Nagelhout

Photo credits: Cover, p. 1 (arrow) Mascha Tace/Shutterstock.com; cover, p. 1 (main) Stockbyte/Stockbyte/
Getty Images; cover, p. 1 (bear) Eric Isselee/Shutterstock.com; ; sidebar used throughout zayats-and-zayats/
Shutterstock.com; background texture used throughout multipear/Shutterstock.com; p. 5 Masao (the straight and
narrow)/Flickr Flash/Getty Images; p. 7 Portland Press Herald/Contributor/Portland Press Herald/Getty Images;
p. 8 Studio DMM Photography, Designs & Art/Shutterstock.com; p. 9 Capricorn4049/Wikimedia Commons;
p. 10 GrahamHardy/Wikimedia Commons; p. 11 Bill Frakes/Contributor/Sports Illustrated/Getty Images;
p. 13 Kansas City Star/Contributor/Tribune News Service/Getty Images; p. 14 Frank Muckenheim/Getty Images;
p. 15 Sea Wave/Shutterstock.com; p. 16 Valentina_S/Shutterstock.com; p. 17 Julien_N/Shutterstock.com;
p. 18 (pig) Potapov Alexander/Shutterstock.com; p. 18 (garbage) vilax/Shutterstock.com; p. 19 US National Archives
bot/Wikimedia Commons; p. 20 Alison Hancock/Shutterstock.com; p. 21 dmitrymoi/Shutterstock.com; p. 22 zokru/
Shutterstock.com; p. 23 Chicago History Museum/Archive Photos/Getty Images; p. 24 Andy Dean Photography/
Shutterstock.com; p. 25 Alfgar/Shutterstock.com; p. 26 Alan.hawk/Wikimedia Commons; p. 27 wonderisland/
Shutterstock.com; p. 28 Iakov Filimonov/Shutterstock.com; p. 29 (false teeth) SasPartout/Shutterstock.com;
p. 29 (fish hook) Julian Rovagnati/Shutterstock.com; p. 29 (ring) Art_girl/Shutterstock.com; p. 29 (coins) Jerry J. Paden/
Shutterstock.com; p. 29 (mustache) Mediagram/Shutterstock.com; p. 29 (pants) Nisakorn Neera/Shutterstock.com.

All rights reserved. No part of this book may be reproduced in any form without permission in writing from
the publisher, except by a reviewer.

Printed in the United States of America

CPSIA compliance information: Batch #CW16GS: For further information contact Gareth Stevens, New York, New York at 1-800-542-2595.

CONTENTS

Words in the glossary appear in **bold** type the first time they are used in the text.

WEIRD GOVERNING

In the United States, laws govern our lives. There are laws for many different things—from laws telling us to wear seat belts in cars and not litter outside to those governing how restaurants prepare our food. While most laws are common sense, there are many parts of life we often don't think about. These laws are meant to protect us from harm and from the actions of others.

Without laws, our world would be a mess! There's usually a good reason for a law being in place. Sometimes, however, laws can be strange—and even funny. Let's explore the odd side of laws!

You Can't Bring What to the Movies?

In Baltimore, Maryland, it's illegal to take a lion to the movies. There isn't much information about why this law exists, so we can only imagine why it was put on the books in the first place. Do you think someone really took a lion to the movies?

There are other strange laws throughout the country about where animals can or can't go. In Sterling, Colorado, cats may not roam freely unless they're wearing a taillight.

5

COLLECTING SEAWEED

Have you ever been to New Hampshire? Make sure you don't take any seaweed called rockweed from the state's beaches at night. Under a New Hampshire state law written in 1973, it's illegal to carry away "seaweed or rockweed from the seashore below high-water mark," which occurs at night.

Some people actually search ocean waters for seaweed like many others do for fish! The seaweed and rockweed are used in animal food and **fertilizer** and are a source of something called alginate, which is used to make liquids thicker. Many people say taking the seaweed hurts ocean animal homes, which explains the law.

Maine, Too?

In Maine, seaweed harvesting has led to a **debate** between those who make money from the harvest and those who say the harvest hurts the ocean. In fact, Maine's state legislature has passed laws on seaweed collection as well. Who knew seaweed was such a hot topic?

rockweed

It's illegal to harvest
seaweed at certain times
in New Hampshire.

7

NO FERRETING ALLOWED

Among the hunting **regulations** in West Virginia is a law preventing hunters from using ferrets to catch their game. According to the law, anyone who uses a ferret to "hunt, catch, take, kill, injure or pursue a wild animal or wild bird" faces a fine and possible jail time. Fines can be as much as $500, and the hunter can face up to 100 days in jail!

But how would you use a ferret to hunt? Called ferreting, the hunter places the animal in a rabbit hole. Then the ferret chases the rabbit out of the hole, and it's easier to catch.

Ferreting doesn't always work, though. Sometimes, the ferret falls asleep in the rabbit's den!

No Drones Either

West Virginia has many different hunting rules. One proposed law would make it illegial for hunters to use unmanned flying machines, often called drones, when hunting animals. Drones would also not be allowed to herd animals, or make them move to a certain area where it's easier to hunt them. Hunters couldn't even use drones to move any already hunted animals!

drone

FROG JUMPING

Every May, the Calaveras County Fair and Jumping Frog **Jubilee** is held in Angels Camp, California. Bullfrog-jumping teams from all over the state come to take part in the event. Over the years, the state has developed laws to make sure the bullfrogs are treated **humanely**.

One law states that frogs that die during the competition can't be eaten or used for any other purpose and must be destroyed as soon as possible. The law may have made its way onto the books as a way to protect people who wanted to compete from legal trouble!

Twain's Beginnings

According to legend, author Mark Twain, who lived in a cabin south of Angels Camp in Calaveras County, wrote his first published work, "The Celebrated Jumping Frog of Calaveras County," after hearing about the frog-jumping contests at a local tavern. Twain wrote the story in 1865, and it received national attention.

People can own as many jumping frogs as they want, but they aren't allowed to eat them if something goes wrong!

11

BINGO!

Have you ever played bingo? For certain groups in North Carolina, a bingo gathering can last no longer than 5 hours. Other **restrictions** make it illegal to hold more than one bingo gathering in 48 hours and to offer prizes higher than $500.

So why do these rules for bingo exist? The game is a form of **gambling**, and the laws try to control the game. The first laws allowing bingo were written in 1945, when the game was permitted at the Mecklenburg County Fair. In 1979, a statewide law allowed charitable organizations to hold bingo games and also permitted unregulated games with prizes under $10.

North Carolina Weird

North Carolina has many other weird laws. Topsail Beach, a small beachfront town, has a local ordinance, or law, against severe storms called hurricanes! The city of Charlotte has an ordinance that says women must cover their body with 16 yards (14.6 m) of cloth at all times!

Ordinances are usually passed for a good reason, but a hurricane can't be stopped by a law!

13

BETTER BE BUTTER

In Iowa, it's illegal to tell people that margarine is butter. In fact, it's a **misdemeanor**! In Wisconsin, it's illegal to serve margarine to customers at a restaurant, hospital, or school, or to prisoners. If a customer asks for margarine, they can have it. Otherwise, it has to be butter.

In the prisons, only the head of a prison can order margarine. The laws are in place to let consumers know what they're eating and give them the choice of having margarine. Food service is highly regulated in the United States, and often for good reason. But this law seems a little strange. Do you think Wisconsin's dairy industry impacted the passage of this law?

margarine

Many people think margarine and butter are the same thing, but don't tell the people in Iowa or Wisconsin that!

butter

What's the Difference?

Butter is made mostly from cow's milk. Margarine has some milk in it, but it also includes vegetable oil. The butter versus margarine debate has been going on for years. Some say margarine is better for you, while others argue that butter is the healthier choice.

PIG PROTECTION

Games that involve catching an oiled or greased-up pig are illegal in Minnesota. According to the law, it's also illegal to play games in which a chicken or turkey "is released or thrown into the air and wherein the object is the capture of the chicken or turkey."

Some say games that involve catching animals are scary for the animals and are inhumane. They think it's wrong that the animals are forced to "play" these games because they have no say in the matter. The animals can also suffer injuries.

Game Over

St. Patrick Parish in Wisconsin came under fire after the church's "pig rassle" fundraiser got lots of attention. The event involved people chasing a pig in a mud pit and trying to touch part of the pig to the top of a barrel. It was last held in 2014, but the parish held a different event in 2015.

Protesters say the pigs were kicked, jumped on, and hurt during the pig rassle event.

17

In Arizona, you can't go around feeding other people's pigs. Pigs are omnivores, which means they eat both plants and animals. They eat lots of different foods—including **garbage**! It's against the law to feed garbage to a swine, another name for a pig, unless you have a permit for it. The pig feeder also needs to apply for that permit every January!

The rule, however, doesn't apply if a person is only feeding their own garbage to their own pig. So if you have your own pig, you can feed it as much scraps and trash as you want!

History of Garbage

Pigs have a long history of eating people's garbage. Many people have kept pigs in their home as pets. These pigs would eat garbage to keep things clean! Some businesses would even have pigs around to eat waste. Pigs are very smart and find food in many places, even our trash!

Some pigs in **medieval** Europe would roam the city searching for food. They even killed children! The pigs were often put on trial for their crimes.

STEALING RAIN?

Up until 2009, it was illegal to collect raindrops in a rain barrel in Colorado. Why was it illegal? According to state law at the time, rain was owned by the state, and anyone taking the rain was stealing from the government!

Weirdly, rain-collecting equipment—like rain barrels—was still sold in the state. People selling rain barrels didn't ask why the equipment was being purchased, and people buying it didn't have to give a reason for buying it! The laws weren't usually enforced, but now people can legally collect rainwater for their personal use.

In Nearby States

Colorado wasn't the only state where collecting rainwater was illegal. In fact, the practice is still illegal in Utah, unless the homeowner owns water rights for the property. In nearby New Mexico, however, many new homes must collect and use rainwater to grow lawns and gardens.

Owning water rights means a person has the right to decide how to use water on or under a piece of land.

CAN'T BEAR IT

Purchasing and training a bear for wrestling is illegal in Alabama and could lead to **felony** charges. Punishment includes fines and paying **restitution** to a humane society. Why would anyone buy a bear and train it to wrestle? Bear wrestling was a popular form of entertainment in the 1800s.

Unfortunately, preparing a bear for wrestling usually meant having its teeth and claws removed or cutting its arm and leg **tendons**. This was done so people wrestling the bear couldn't be hurt badly, but it was very painful for the bears. That's why the law was passed.

Bears in Cars

If a person leaves food in a car and a bear breaks in to eat it, a park ranger can give the car owner a ticket! In 2014, a woman in Washington was pulled over for speeding in the carpool lane. She got another ticket when the officer saw she had a giant teddy bear in the passenger's seat instead of another person!

black bear

Many declawed bears wrestled at state fairs, like the one pictured here. Terrible Ted was a famous American black bear that traveled with circuses during the 1950s.

NO BILLBOARDS HERE

Have you ever noticed how many billboards dot the landscape when you're driving on the highway? They're all over the place! But you won't find any in Hawaii. There, billboards are illegal! The law dates back to the 1920s and still has supporters. A group called the Outdoor Circle still works with the government to keep Hawaii billboard-free.

Several other states, including Alaska, Maine, and Vermont, also ban billboards. Not everyone likes the ban, though. Small business owners especially say it hurts them because they can't advertise!

There are 18 exceptions to the billboard ban, including voting signs, "for sale" signs, and "now hiring" signs. Big billboards still aren't allowed, though!

Tourism is a huge industry for Hawaii, so businesses are limited in what kinds of signs they can use to block the scenery.

Kuaui, Hawaii

Natural Beauty

The Outdoor Circle also works to keep power lines underground on the islands instead of having them block scenic views. This can cost companies more money, but the group insists. The group maintains that Hawaii is best served by preserving its natural beauty.

THE FOOT-O-SCOPE

How do you figure out your shoe size? You probably didn't take an X ray of your foot. It sounds strange, but there used to be a machine called a Foot-O-Scope, which used special rays to look at the bones of your foot to figure out its size.

Radiation from X rays is dangerous for humans, so shoe sellers stopped using the machines. Nevada, however, actually put a law on the books making it illegal. New York State passed a law in 1948 that said children couldn't use it more than 12 times a year.

The Foot-O-Scope turned out to be a bad idea—and dangerous.

Foot-O-Scope

X Rays

X rays use radiation to create pictures of bones. The rays are waves of radiation that pass through your body. Special machines can make pictures that show bones and other dense matter, but look through other parts of your body. Today's X rays are much safer than the early ones used in the Foot-O-Scope.

27

FACT OR FICTION?

Not all the weird laws you may read about or hear about are actually true. There are stories claiming it's illegal to have an ice cream cone in your back pocket in Alabama or for children to have a weird haircut in Texas. Some websites even claim there's a California law stating that you're not allowed to ride a bike in a swimming pool.

Sometimes, if a law sounds too silly to be true, it actually is! Keep that in mind the next time you hear about a strange new law that just doesn't seem to make sense.

Arizona Lies

Some states have dozens of stories about laws that don't actually exist. In Arizona, for example, there are stories about laws that make suspenders illegal in certain towns. Other stories tell of laws that limit the hunting of camels or ban women from wearing pants! But these are just stories, not laws!

EVEN MORE ODD LAWS

Vermont
Women must get permission from their husband to wear false teeth

Montana
Married women cannot go fishing alone on Sundays

Alabama
No wearing of fake mustaches in church

Phoenix, Arizona
Any man entering the city must be wearing pants

Hawaii
No placing of coins in the ears

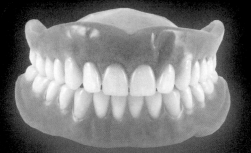

GLOSSARY

debate: an argument between two sides

felony: a serious crime punishable by lengthy jail time

fertilizer: material added to soil to make plants grow bigger

gambling: the act of playing games and betting money on them

garbage: food or other matter that has been thrown away

humanely: marked by sympathy or consideration for others

jubilee: a special event

medieval: relating to the Middle Ages, a period in European history from about 500 to about 1500

misdemeanor: a less serious crime punished by jail time or a fine

radiation: energy created and moved in the form of waves or particles

regulation: a rule or order having the force of law

restitution: the act of paying something back of equal value for some harm

restriction: something that limits

tendon: a tough cord or band of tissue that connects muscle with bone

FOR MORE INFORMATION

BOOKS

Cocotos, Tom Nick. *Weird But True! Stupid Criminals: 150 Brainless Baddies Busted, Plus Wacky Facts.* Washington, DC: National Geographic, 2012.

Morgan, Matthew. *Children's Miscellany: Useless Information That's Essential to Know.* San Francisco, CA: Chronicle Books, 2005.

WEBSITES

Dumb Laws
dumblaws.com
Weird laws from all over the United States, searchable by state.

USA.gov Laws
usa.gov/laws-and-regulations
Find out more about some of the most important national laws here.

Publisher's note to educators and parents: Our editors have carefully reviewed these websites to ensure that they are suitable for students. Many websites change frequently, however, and we cannot guarantee that a site's future contents will continue to meet our high standards of quality and educational value. Be advised that students should be closely supervised whenever they access the Internet.

INDEX